D0986470

# WHEN GOD SPEAKS, YOU BETTER LISTEN!

by

## Nan Clark

**Copyright © 2017 by Nan Clark**

# ACKNOWLEDGMENTS

Special thanks to Msgr. John J. Graham {Pastor of St. Frances de Chantal Church, Bronx, NY) for his in-depth reading of the text; to Margie DiSilvio  and Mary Moussot (longtime members of the St. Frances Prayer Group) for their thoughtful suggestions and constant encouragement; to Bill Braem for his technological expertise, and to Deacon John Murphy for his imaginative contribution to the cover.

Nan Clark

July 2021

# CONTENTS

# PART I

# RESPONDING TO GOD'S COMMANDS

## LESSON: Saying "Yes" to God Calls for OBEDIENCE

The Judeo-Christian belief in God's gift of free will is told in the Biblical[1] story of Adam and Eve in the Garden of Eden. By eating fruit from the forbidden tree of the knowledge of good and evil, Adam and Eve disobeyed their Creator (Genesis 2:15-17; 3:1-6) and yielded to the serpent's[2] lie that eating the fruit would make them as powerful as God.

With their banishment from the Garden, the consequences of their action were passed down to all humanity, with the exception of the Blessed Virgin Mary. Sin, suffering, and death entered the world together with an ever-present conflict between good and evil.

Throughout history, God's greatest adversary has tried to seduce humans into believing that it's all right to ignore or reject God's commands. But it isn't! God punishes sinners who do not repent, but God also forgives those who do. Time and again, in His infinite love, wisdom, and mercy, Our Creator has sent angels, prophets, and saints; Jesus, Mary, and the Holy Spirit, and those special people in our lives to help us stay on the road to everlasting life.

---

[1] All Biblical references are from *The New American Bible, Revised Edition (NABRE)*, 2010.

[2] The serpent symbolizes the devil. (Revelation 12:9)

# THREE OLD TESTAMENT PATRIARCHS

## 1. NOAH: GOD'S FAITHFUL SERVANT

## A. LESSON: Saying "Yes" to God Calls for PERSEVERANCE

*The Bible* tells us that as the population of the earth increased, so did the number of people who turned away from God. As punishment for their evil ways, God decided to cause a great flood which would destroy everyone and everything on the face of the earth. (Genesis 6:7)

But God was pleased with one man, whose name was Noah. Before the waters came, He told Noah to build an ark which would house himself, his family, and a male and female member of each animal species that he could find.

After God gave Noah the dimensions of the vessel, Noah set to work. Imagine the ridicule he had to face when he told onlookers what he was doing and why, but because Noah obeyed his Creator, God gave humanity another chance to serve Him.

On seeing the devastation that the flood waters had caused, God promised that He would never again send a flood to destroy the earth and all its living creatures. (Genesis 8:21) He then placed a rainbow in the sky as the visible sign of the covenant He had made with Noah. (Genesis 9:13)

## B. QUESTIONS for Personal Reflection and/or Group Discussion

1. How did Noah handle obstacles, criticism, and ridicule?

_____

_____

_____

_____

2. How <u>do</u> I handle obstacles, criticism, and ridicule?

_____

_____

_____

_____

3. How <u>should</u> I handle obstacles, criticism, and ridicule?

_____

_____

_____

_____

# 2. ABRAHAM: "FATHER OF MANY NATIONS"

## A. LESSON: Saying "Yes" to God Calls for SACRIFICE

Another person with whom God made a covenant was Abraham, a descendant of Noah's son Shem. Originally named Abram, God commanded him to leave his home, relatives, and country and go to a new land, a land which his offspring would inherit. (Genesis 12:1;7) Abram obeyed.

Although Abram's wife, Sarai, was well beyond her child-bearing years, God kept referring to their descendants as countless as the stars in the sky and the grains of sand on the seashore. Abram put his trust in the Lord: He believed that with God all things are possible.

When Abram and Sarai were nearly 100 years old, Sarai became pregnant with Isaac.[1] God then changed Abram's name to Abraham, for he was to be "A Blessing to Others" and "The Father of Many Nations." (Genesis 17:5) God also changed Sarai's name to Sarah ("Princess"). [2] (Genesis 17:15)

God then told Abraham that the sign of His new covenant with humanity would be circumcision, a personal and visible means to "mark God's own." Abraham promised that he and all his descendants - every male - whether born within the household or bought - would be circumcised. (Genesis 17:10 -11)

The ultimate test of Abraham's obedience to God occurred when God told him to sacrifice his son Isaac. As Abraham was about to kill the boy, God provided an animal offering instead. What Abraham intended to do shows that his obedience to God's will was more important than his love for any person or thing on earth. (God asks each one of us to have that same trust in His plan for our lives).

---

[1] Although Abraham had an older son named Ishmael with Sarah's Egyptian maid-servant Hagar, it was Isaac who was Abraham's legitimate heir. Nevertheless, God also blessed Ishmael by giving him many children and making a great nation of his descendants. (Genesis 17:20)

[2] God also changed the name of Isaac's son Jacob to Israel. (Genesis 32:29) Jacob's descendants are the Israelites.

## B. **QUESTIONS** for Personal Reflection and/or Group Discussion

1. What was Abraham asked to give up?

_____

_____

_____

_____

2. How did Abraham feel about doing this?

_____

_____

_____

_____

3. Were you ever asked to give something up? What?

_____

4. Did you give it up voluntarily or were you forced to relinquish it?

_____

5. How did this make you feel?

_____

_____

_____

_____

# 3. <u>MOSES: LEADER OF THE ISRAELITES</u>

A. <u>LESSON</u>: Saying "Yes" to God Calls for **TOTAL ACCEPTANCE OF GOD'S AUTHORITY**

Hundreds of years later, well after the death of many of Abraham's descendants who had lived and prospered in Egypt, the current Pharaoh turned on the Israelites and began treating them like slaves. God (Who has always intervened in human history) decided that the time had come for His chosen people to go to a land of their own, and He selected an Israelite named Moses as their leader.

Moses protested to God that it just wasn't enough to refer to Him as the God of Abraham, Isaac, and Jacob; he needed God's name so that the Israelites would accept what he would tell them. "God replied to Moses: 'I am who I am.' Then He added: 'This is what you will tell the Israelites: I AM[1] has sent me to you.' (Exodus 3:14) "This is my name forever; this is my title for all generations." (Exodus 3:15)

God then sent Moses to the Pharaoh ten times with the same request: "Let my people go." Each time the Pharaoh refused and each time God launched a plague upon the Egyptians. The last plague was the worst of all. It was the death of every Egyptian's firstborn son and firstborn male domestic animal. The Israelites and their livestock were spared because God had instructed them to sprinkle some blood on the lintel and two doorposts of their homes. This blood was to be taken from a one-year-old unblemished goat or sheep whose bones had not been broken. In this way the "Angel of Death" would see the blood and pass over[2] their houses. (Exodus 12: 1-13) God also instructed the Israelites to be dressed for flight as they ate the roasted flesh of the sacrificed animal with unleavened bread and bitter herbs.

---

[1]·Since the original Hebrew language contains no vowels, God's name, "I AM" is written YHWH. This has come down to us as Yahweh.
[2]·Hence, the Jewish feast of Passover.

# 1. <u>THE FLIGHT FROM EGYPT</u>

When the Pharaoh saw the most recent effects of Yahweh's horrific power, he relented and allowed the Israelites to leave Egyptian soil. But the Pharaoh did not relent for long. He soon sent horses, chariots, horsemen, and an army of soldiers after them. Under Moses' command the Israelites approached the Red Sea with the Egyptian forces in hot pursuit. Then the LORD, Who had been traveling with His chosen people in a pillar of cloud by day and a pillar of fire by night, told Moses to raise his staff and stretch his arm over the water. As soon as Moses did this, the water receded and a corridor of dry land with a wall of water on either side opened before the Israelites. Then the Egyptians entered the water. When they were well into the corridor, Moses lowered his arm and the water rose and flowed over them, causing every man and beast in Pharaoh's army to drown.

As the result of God's mighty deeds, the Israelites put their trust in the LORD.

# 2. <u>"THE TEN COMMANDMENTS"</u>

Our loving Creator has given us the gift of free will so that we might choose to love Him as He loves us. We show that love by obeying His laws. Recognizing that both the gift of free will and our fallen nature can weaken our resolve to live in an ever-present loving relationship with God and each other, Yahweh summoned Moses to climb Mount Sinai to receive a set of ten rules to help us stay on the right path. Written by the "finger of God" (Exodus 31:18) on two stone tablets, and known as "The Ten Commandments," this visible sign of Yahweh's covenant with Moses and the Israelites tells God's chosen people what is expected of them.[1]

---

[1] The first three Commandments focus on our relationship with God; the remaining Commandments focus on our relationship with our neighbor.

**The emphasis in these commandments is on the <u>Don'ts</u>.**

| <u>Should NOT Do</u> | <u>Should Do</u> |
|---|---|
| I. I, the LORD, am your God. You shall not have other gods besides Me. | 3. Remember to keep holy the LORD's day. |
| 2. You shall not take the name of the LORD GOD in vain. | 4. Honor your father and your mother. |
| 5. You shall not kill. | |
| 6. You shall not commit adultery. | |
| 7. You shall not steal. | |
| 8. You shall not bear false witness. | |
| 9. You shall not covet your neighbor's wife. | |
| 10. You shall not covet your neighbor's goods. | |

The LORD then instructed Moses to write an explanation of how these rules should be applied in different situations. It took Moses 40 days and 40 nights, without eating or drinking, to do as Yahweh had commanded.

During the time that Moses spent atop Mount Sinai, the Israelites down below turned to idol worship because they felt abandoned by both Yahweh and Moses.

Seeing this on his return, Moses became so infuriated that he smashed the tablets to bits. When Yahweh saw what Moses had done, He said to him, "Cut two stone tablets like the first ones, and I will write on them the words that were on the first tablets, which you broke. Place them in an ark you are to make out of acacia wood."[1] (Deut. 10:1-2) Then Yahweh told Moses that He was going to destroy the Israelites and make Moses the leader of another people.

_____

[1] Just as God had given Noah the dimensions of the Ark he was to build, God now gave Moses the dimensions of the Ark of the Covenant, which was to house "The Ten Commandments."

For the next 40 days and nights, Moses prostrated himself before Yahweh atop Mount Sinai, neither eating nor drinking, but constantly appealing to Him to forego the punishment He was going to mete out. Yahweh finally relented, and renewed the covenants He had made with Moses and his forefathers. Moses then descended from Mount Sinai with the second set of "The Ten Commandments" in a sealed box.

Appearing before the assembled Israelites, he spoke these words:

> "Now, therefore, Israel, what does the LORD, your
> God, ask of you but to fear the LORD, your God, to
> follow in all His ways, to love and serve the LORD, your God,
> with your whole heart and with your whole being, to keep
> the commandments and statutes of the LORD that I
> am commanding you today for your own well-being?"[2]
> (Deuteronomy 10:12-13)

---

[2] In the New Testament, when Jesus was asked which commandment was the most important, He confirmed what God had revealed to Moses and the Israelites on Mount Sinai: **"You shall love the LORD, your God, with all your heart, with all your soul, and with all your mind. This is the greatest and the first commandment."** (Matthew 22:34-38) And then, Jesus summed up the other nine commandments: "The second is like it: You shall love your neighbor as yourself. The whole law and the prophets depend on these two commandments." (Matthew 22:39-40)

14

**B. <u>QUESTIONS</u>** for Personal Reflection and/or Group Discussion

1. What did God tell Moses to do?

_____

_____

_____

_____

2. Which Commandment(s) do you find most difficult to practice?

a. _____

_____

Why? _____

_____

_____

_____

b. _____

_____

Why? _____

_____

_____

_____

3. What do you think could be of help to you in this situation?

_____

_____

_____

_____

4. Have you accepted God in your life?

_____

5. How are you trying to accept God in your life?

_____

_____

_____

_____

6. What do you think God is telling you to do?

_____

_____

_____

_____

# PART II

**LESSON:** Saying "Yes" to God Calls for **PROCLAIMING GOD'S WORD**

# THREE OLD TESTAMENT PROPHETS

## 1. JEREMIAH: GOD'S MOST INSECURE SPOKESPERSON

### A. LESSON: Saying "Yes" to God Calls for TRUST

Throughout salvation history God has chosen both likely and unlikely individuals to deliver His messages, and some of His spokespeople, like Jonah, Moses, and Jeremiah,[1] did not want the job. Jonah ran away and Moses[2] and Jeremiah offered reasons why they weren't qualified. Nevertheless, God prevailed.

Jeremiah had to be convinced of his worthiness. He tells us:

> "The word of the LORD came to me:
> 'Before I formed you in the womb, I knew you;
> Before you were born, I dedicated you;
> A prophet to the nations, I appointed you.'"

> "Ah, LORD GOD!" I said,
> "I do not know how to speak;
> I am too young!" (Jeremiah 1:4-6)

> Then the LORD extended his hand
> And touched my mouth, saying to me,

> "See, I place my words in your mouth!
> Today I appoint you over nations and over kingdoms,
> To uproot and to tear down, to destroy and to demolish,
> To build and to plant." (Jeremiah 1:9 -10)

---

[1] Jeremiah is called "The Weeping Prophet" because of all the bad things he foresaw. His writings are found in the **Old Testament** *Book of Jeremiah* and, according to tradition, in some of the poetic presentations in *The Book of Lamentations*. Jeremiah is also known for his Messianic prophecies.

[2] Moses also claimed to be "slow of speech and tongue," but God said He would give His messages to Moses and use his brother Aaron to deliver them. (Exodus 4:16)

In exactly the same way that the LORD knew Jeremiah, so, too, does He know each one of us. As with Jeremiah, before He formed us, before we were born, the LORD dedicated us to accomplish a certain task here on earth, and regardless of how many excuses we offer for our weaknesses and inabilities, God wants us to carry out what He has given each one of us to do – but we still have free will to obey Him or not!

As with Jeremiah, when we do make that commitment to serve Him, God will work wonders in us and for us! He will always be present to help and guide us.

## B. <u>QUESTIONS</u> for Personal Reflection and/or Group Discussion

1. Although Jeremiah felt unworthy and lacked self-confidence, God called him to be a prophet.

   What do you think God has called you to be/do?

   _____

   _____

   _____

   _____

2. What excuse/s did/do you make when you were/are confronted with a situation you didn't/don't want to be involved in?

   _____

   _____

   _____

   _____

3. Can you think of a more effective way of handling this kind of situation?

_____

_____

_____

_____

# 2. JONAH: GOD'S MOST REBELLIOUS MESSENGER

## A. LESSON: Saying "Yes" to God Calls for REPENTANCE, CONVERSION, AND FORGIVENESS

God called Jonah to go to Nineveh to preach repentance to its inhabitants for their wicked ways, but Jonah didn't want to go. Instead, he boarded a ship which was headed in the opposite direction. (But you can't get away from God)!

When a storm came up, Jonah knew it was God's way of punishing him for his disobedience, so he asked the sailors to throw him overboard so that he alone would perish. When they did as he requested, he was swallowed by a great fish and after three days and three nights in its belly, he was spit out and found himself back in his own country.

Once again, the LORD told Jonah to go to Nineveh, and this time Jonah obeyed. His preaching was so effective that all the inhabitants of Nineveh repented. Seeing this, the LORD decided not to carry out the punishment He had intended, but Jonah was angry at the LORD's decision. He wanted the people of Nineveh to pay for their disobedience to God. Jonah did not see that just as God had given him a second chance to obey His command, He was now giving the repentant Ninevites a second chance to reform their lives. Jonah wanted justice, but God granted mercy.

As always, God prevailed.

## B. QUESTIONS for Personal Reflection and/or Group Discussion

Jonah is judgmental: He even tells God what to do.

He wants "Pay Back" even after repentance.

1. Have you ever told God what to do?  When?  Why?

_____

_____

_____

_____

2. Have you <u>completely</u> forgiven those who have hurt you?

_____

_____

_____

_____

3. Have you sought forgiveness from those you have hurt?

_____

_____

4. How do you understand the statement: "I will forgive, but I'll never forget."?

_____

_____

_____

_____

# 3. <u>ISAIAH: GOD'S MOST WILLING EMISSARY</u>

## A. <u>LESSON</u>: Saying "Yes" to God Calls for **PATIENT ENDURANCE**

The prophet Isaiah (whose name means "Salvation of the LORD") lived in Judah, Israel's Southern kingdom, from the middle of the 8th century BCE to the beginning of the 7th century BCE. It was a time of many wars and great turmoil. Isaiah, who was consumed by the majesty, power, and splendor of God, was keenly aware of the great divide between the holiness of God and the sinfulness of His people.

In one of his visions, Isaiah saw the Almighty seated on His throne, surrounded by angels chanting: "Holy, holy, holy is the Lord of hosts! All the earth is filled with His glory!" (Isaiah 6:3), This experience prompted Isaiah to ask the LORD to be cleansed of his sins so that he might serve Him with a pure heart.

At this time in Israel's history, God was so displeased with the evil ways of His chosen people that He decided to send a messenger to warn them that they would be severely punished if they did not repent. Isaiah yearned to be that messenger. When God asked, "Whom shall I send? Who will go for us?" Isaiah responded: "Here I am; send me!" (Isaiah 6:8) And God did!

Throughout salvation history God keeps telling us that He will deal harshly with sinners, but mercifully with those who repent. In Isaiah 1:18-20, for example, we read:

> "Come now, let us set things right," says the LORD:
> "Though your sins be like scarlet, they may become white as snow;
> Though they be red like crimson, they may become white as wool.
> If you are willing, and obey, you shall eat the good things of the land;
> But if you refuse and resist, you shall be eaten by the sword
> For the mouth of the LORD has spoken!"

Although Isaiah preached God's message, most people rejected it, and bad times continued. Still, God gave hope to Israel's faithful remnant by promising to send them a savior, a redeemer, a messiah who would suffer for the sins of humanity, be resurrected from the dead, and eventually establish an everlasting kingdom of peace on earth.

Isaiah's detailed prophecies about the coming of Jesus greatly outnumber those found in any other book of **The Bible**.

## B. **QUESTIONS** for Personal Reflection and/or Group Discussion

1. Isaiah was Impulsive. He wanted to go everywhere and do everything Immediately.
   Are you that way? Explain.

   _____

   _____

   _____

   _____

2. Did you ever feel that God was asking you to be His messenger: to give someone a word of comfort, hope, encouragement, support, consolation, advice, warning, etc.?
   If so, what was your response? Then what happened? Explain.

   _____

   _____

   _____

   _____

3. Did you ever fail as a "Do Gooder" because you acted too quickly, without planning your strategy? Explain.

   _____

   _____

   _____

   _____

# PART III

# ST. PAUL: GOD'S FEARLESS PREACHER OF THE NEW TESTAMENT

## A. <u>LESSON</u>: Saying "Yes" to God Calls for
## <u>EMBRACING HARDSHIP</u>

## (One cannot strengthen others unless one is strong him/herself).

Not only has God chosen both divine and human messengers to proclaim His word, instruct the faithful, strengthen the fainthearted, help those in need, and warn those in danger about possible future events, but He also uses all kinds of ways to make us listen to Him. In the New Testament, for example, God spoke to Saul (also known as Paul) through a direct encounter with Jesus. For Saul, this confrontation was a life-changing event. It occurred on what turned out to be Saul's final mission: rounding up Jews who were Christ-followers and sending them to jail.

When Jesus identified Himself as the One Saul was persecuting, Saul fell to the ground and on rising, was unable to see. Jesus instructed him to go to Damascus, to the house of a man named Judas, where he would be visited by a man named Ananias, who would lay hands on him, and his sight would be restored. Saul obeyed Jesus' command and went to Judas' house. After he had fasted for three days, Ananias appeared and Saul regained his sight. Then he was baptized. (Acts 9:4-19)

With even greater zeal and enthusiasm than he had shown as a Pharisee[1] persecuting the Jewish followers of Jesus, Saul became totally dedicated to the Son of God and His teachings.[2] (Acts 13:9) He decided that his special mission was to bring Jesus to people who weren't Jewish -- the Gentiles.

---

[1] A strict observer of Jewish law, implying, therefore, that this type of person is holier than other people.

[2] Because of his past deeds, however, there were those -- especially among the Christianized Jews and even the apostles -- who questioned Paul's sincerity, and there were others who wanted him dead.

24

Despite the many hardships he had to face, Paul never wavered in his commitment to spread the Good News. Through his inspired writings, impassioned preaching, and extensive travel, he soon became known as "Paul, Apostle to the Gentiles."

## B. <u>QUESTIONS</u> for Personal Reflection and/or Group Discussion

1. What kept Paul going?

_____

_____

_____

_____

2. Did you ever have a "conversion" experience? <u>Explain</u>.

_____

_____

_____

_____

3. How did people react to you after your "conversion?"

_____

_____

_____

_____

4. After your "conversion" how did you react to people? <u>Explain</u>.

_____

_____

_____

_____

# PART IV

## EXPERIENCING THE INEXPLICABLE

## A. THE EUCHARIST[*1]

### 1. A Brief History

When God dwelt among us in human form as Jesus, He subjected Himself to an earthly life span of 33 years and an agonizing death by crucifixion in atonement for the sins of humanity. Nevertheless, Jesus promised that He would always be with us.

It was at the Passover[2] meal on the night He was arrested that Jesus said to the apostles: "From now on I am telling you before it happens, so that when it happens, you may believe **I AM**."[3]

---

[1.] Eucharist is a Greek word which means "Thanksgiving."

[2.] In 33 CE, the first day of Passover fell on a Thursday, which Christians continue to celebrate on this day of the week as "Holy Thursday" or "The Last Supper." According to the Jewish calendar, each year Passover begins on a different day of the week.

[3.] **I AM** is the name of the triune God, which the Father (the first person of the Holy Trinity) revealed to Moses. (Exodus 3:13-14) When Jesus says, "**I AM**," He is proclaiming His divinity as God the Son (the second Person of the Holy Trinity). God the Holy Spirit (the third Person of the Holy Trinity) was first mentioned to the apostles at the Last Supper: "Amen, amen, I say to you, whoever receives the One I send **(the Holy Spirit)** receives Me **(Jesus)**, and whoever receives Me **(Jesus)**, receives the One Who sent Me **(the Father)**." (John 13:19-20)

26

Then He blessed the bread and the wine, which He gave to them, saying,

"Take this, all of you, and eat of it,
for this is my Body,
which will be given up for you.
Take this, all of you, and drink from it,
for this is the chalice of my Blood,
the Blood of the new and eternal covenant
which will be poured out for you and for many
for the forgiveness of sins.
Do this in memory of me."

Catholics believe that with these words, ordinary bread and wine are transformed into the actual flesh and blood of Jesus Christ. This prayer signals the most solemn moments in a Catholic Mass. It is said as the priest elevates the bread and the wine and invites the faithful to partake of Jesus.

John quotes Jesus' actual words: "Whoever eats my flesh and drinks my blood has eternal life, and I will raise him on the last day; for my flesh is true food, and my blood is true drink." (John 6:54-55)

# 2. <u>The Eucharistic Miracle in Lanciano, Italy (750)</u>

In the year 750 A.D. in the Church of St. Longinus[1] in Lanciano, Italy, Jesus' flesh and blood actually became visible. This miracle occurred in response to the skepticism of one of the priests who questioned whether or not Jesus was truly present during the consecration of the bread and wine. Even after 13 centuries, Jesus' flesh and blood may still be seen in their original state.[2]

**750 A.D.
Lanciano, Italy**

**Below the heart arteries and veins can be easily identified, as well as a double slender branch of the vagus nerve.**

*The Flesh and Blood of Lanciano therefore are just the same as they would be if they had been drawn that very day from a living human being.*

The conservation of the Flesh and the Blood, left in their natural state of twelve centuries and exposed to the influence of atmospheric and biological elements, remains an extraordinary phenomenon.
(The Linoli Report - 4/13/1971)

---

[1] According to traditional legends, Longinus was the Roman soldier who thrust his spear into Jesus' side at the crucifixion.

In 1258, the Church of St. Longinus in Lanciano, Italy, which housed the Eucharistic miracle, was re-built and re-named *Santuario di San Francesco* in honor of St. Francis of Assisi.

[2] The Miracle in Lanciano. [VIDEO] 4/17/2011
https://www.youtube.com/watch?v=whbzLYi7cyc

Subjected to various scientific tests since 1574, the results of those performed in 1971 confirmed the fact that the Eucharistic flesh in the monstrance is human flesh from the muscular tissue of the heart, and the blood is human blood, type AB. This is the same blood type found on the Burial Shroud of Turin and in other Eucharistic miracles.[3]

---

[3] Miracle of Lanciano Medical Report by Dr. Linoli [VIDEO]9/4/2020.
**https://www.YouTube.com/watch?v=OaoaHNhX1pk**

# 3. The Eucharistic Miracle in Buenos Aires, Argentina (1996)

This is the story of the transformed Host in Buenos Aires, Argentina, when Pope Francis was the city's bishop.

It was on August 18, 1996, at Mass in St. Mary's Catholic Church in the commercial district of the city that a woman went to the end of the Communion line to tell the celebrant, Fr. Alejandro Pezet, that there was a discarded Host in a candlestick stand in the back of the church. Because the Host was dirty, the priest did not consume It, but followed church protocol by putting It in a jar of water, which he then placed inside the tabernacle. When he opened the tabernacle eight days later, he found that the original unleavened white bread Host had turned into a bloody substance. He reported his findings to the proper church authorities, and on September 6, the then Bishop Bergoglio (who became Buenos Aires' archbishop in 1998, cardinal in 2001, and Pope Francis in 2013) had the Host professionally photographed.[1]

---

[1] Pope Francis, Eucharistic Miracle in Buenos Aires, Argentina …
**https://www.absoluteprimacyofchrist.org/pope-francis-eucharistic-miracle-in-buenos-aires-argentina/  Posted March 28, 2013.**

The Host was then placed in a jar of distilled water and returned to the tabernacle, where It remained for the next three years.

By this time the bloody substance had really grown in size. Bishop Bergoglio then called in Dr. Ricardo Castañón, a leading neuropsychophysiologist who was to go with a fragment of the substance to New York for a professional analysis. He was to be accompanied by a lawyer and a journalist. All three men were instructed not to disclose any information about the fragment.

One of the examining team's members was Dr. Frederick Zugibe, a noted cardiologist and forensic pathologist, who was also well-known for his work on crucifixion and the Burial Shroud of Turin. He had also studied thousands of corpses in his position as the first Chief Medical Examiner in New York's Rockland County.

Dr. Zugibe's analysis revealed that the bloody fragment was human flesh from the heart tissue of the left ventricle wall. Deeply embedded in the flesh were white blood cells, which indicated that this person had undergone great stress and suffering. Like the Host from Lanciano, the DNA sample showed an AB positive blood type.

The one thing that Dr. Zugibe could not understand was how the cells in this part of a heart which had first been kept in regular water and then for three years in distilled water, were living, moving, and beating when he examined them. According to the laws of physics, this was impossible. The bishop's representatives then told him the whole story.

# 4. Of Added Interest: *Eucharistic Miracles of the World*

***Eucharistic Miracles of the World*** is a computer program which has not only been presented as an international exhibit, but which can also be viewed at home on a computer screen. In addition to the Miracle at Lanciano, the program contains over 100 documented and catalogued examples of Eucharistic miracles which have taken place in different countries throughout the centuries.[1]

This comprehensive undertaking is the work of Carlo Acutis (1991-2006), an extraordinary boy who, from the time he received his first holy communion at the age of seven, became a computer "geek" in order to dedicate his brief life to evangelizing his love for Jesus in the Holy Eucharist. When Carlo died from leukemia at the age of 15, he was so well-known for his devotion to Our Lord that in 2013, the process for his canonization began. It reached its second stage[2] in 2018 when Pope Francis declared him "Venerable."

On October 10, 2020, Pope Francis declared Carlo "Blessed." His feast day Is October 12.

---

[1] The details for setting up an exhibit and/or viewing the program at home may be found on the website which Carlo created: http://www.**miracolieucaristi**.org

[2] Stage One:  Servant of God
  Stage Two:  Venerable
  Stage Three: Blessed
  Stage Four:  Saint

# B. <u>THE BLESSED MOTHER</u>

Above all the angels and saints who, like God, are ever-present to help us human beings stay on the "high-way" to Heaven, is the Great Mother of God, Mary, Most Holy. Through an extraordinary act of the Almighty, God has given us this special advocate who partakes of the Divine and acts as God's chief human emissary. When the archangel Gabriel told Mary that God had chosen her for a very special purpose, she replied: "Behold, I am the handmaid of the Lord. May it be done to me according to your word." (Luke 1:38)

Mary offered herself in complete surrender to God's will.

As God's foremost heavenly messenger, Mary has revealed many facts about herself and her place in God's kingdom. She has taught us how we are to pray and do penance for the repentance and conversion of sinners. She has warned us about the dire consequences awaiting individuals who do not amend their godless ways. Yet, Mary is always an encourager and a healing presence to those who seek her aid, just as she was in her manifestation as Our Lady of the Pillar.

# 1. <u>OUR LADY OF THE PILLAR</u>

It is believed that Mary's first apparition on earth was to the apostle St. James the Greater[1] in the year 40 CE in Zaragoza, Spain.[2]

Mary was seen at the Ebro River, standing on a six-foot pillar of unknown jasper. She was holding the child Jesus in her left arm and a 15" wooden replica of herself and Jesus in her right arm.

Mary's mission was to console and encourage St. James, who was despondent because he was making so few converts to Jesus. As in many of her future visitations throughout the world, Mary told St. James to begin building a church on the spot where she had appeared. She also instructed him to put the little wooden statue inside the structure.

Not only did that original church grow to become a great basilica, but the 15" wooden statue is still there - and in perfect condition! This Church of Our Lady of the Pillar in Zaragoza, Spain soon became (and still is) one of the world's most popular places of pilgrimage.[3] Mary's little statue, which dates back to the very beginnings of Christianity, is a loving reminder of God's eternal presence among us.

---

[1] There were two apostles named James: James the Just and James the Greater ("Greater" because he was taller than the other James).
James the Greater and his brother John the Evangelist were "The Sons of Thunder" - the offspring of Zebedee and Salome. It was Salome who asked Jesus if her sons could sit at His right hand and His left hand when they got to Heaven.
James the Greater was the first apostle to be martyred.
John was the last apostle to leave this world and the only apostle to die of natural causes.

[2] Jesus told the apostles to go out to the whole world with the message of salvation. James the Greater went to Spain.

[3] Our Lady of the Pillar is the patroness of Spain and of all Hispanic people.
St. James the Greater (Santiago) and St. Teresa of Avila are the patron saints of Spain.
Pilar is a popular girls' name.

# 2. <u>OUR LADY OF GUADALUPE</u>

# a. The Story

To be deemed an actual visitation of the Virgin Mary, the local bishop must conduct a rigorous investigation of everyone and everything associated with the event. Once all the claims are authenticated, the bishop typically gives his approval by stating that this appearance of the Blessed Mother is "worthy of belief."[1]

Although there have been hundreds of local bishop-approved visitations of Mary, there are fewer than 20 that the Vatican has sanctioned as truly divine in origin. One of the most famous occurred near Mexico City in December 1531. Here, the Blessed Mother came down to earth to convert the native Aztec Indians to Christianity. This involved putting an end to their practice of human sacrifice and worship of false gods. Mary appeared four times to a newly-converted Aztec named Juan Diego and once to his dying uncle, Juan Bernardino, whom she cured after scolding Juan Diego for not telling her his need: "Am I not here, I, who am your mother?"[2]

---

[1] Since such happenings are not matters of faith and morals, one does not have to believe in them.

[2] Mary's words to Juan Diego tell us that she is also our heavenly mother. They remind us of Jesus' words on the Cross when He said to John the Apostle, "Behold your mother," and to Mary, "Woman, behold your son."

At their first meeting on Tepayac Hill (which formerly housed a temple of pagan worship dedicated to Tonantzin, the Aztec mother god), Mary told Juan that she was the Mother of the one true God.[3] She instructed him to go to the bishop with this message and the request that a church be built in her honor on the spot where she had appeared.

Bishop Zumárraga told Juan he would think about what he had said. When Juan returned the next day, the bishop asked him to come back again, this time with some sign which would validate his story. After Juan related this to the Blessed Mother, she told him to go to the top of Tepayac Hill and pick some flowers - which he was to put in his tilma[4] and present to the bishop the following day.

The flowers were roses, which were not only not native to the area, but also do not bloom in winter. Even more spectacular than the roses, however, was what was imprinted on the inside of Juan's tilma: the depiction of Mary as a pregnant Aztec princess. This image, which used native Aztec symbolism to show Christianity's superiority over paganism, resulted in nine million Aztec conversions over the next seven years, the greatest mass conversion in human history.[5]

---

[3] In 431, the Council of Ephesus proclaimed the first doctrine about Mary: "Mary, the God Bearer;" "Mary, the Mother of God."

[4] Tilma: A cape made of cactus fiber.

[5] Kioska, Robert. "Why Did Nine Million People Suddenly Turn Catholic?"
Thoughts from the Side of the House
https://sideofthehouse.blog/2017/01/23

# b. <u>What the Image Reveals</u>

The image[6] shows Mary standing in front of the sun, surrounded by its rays. Her position convinced the pagans of her supremacy over Huitzilopochtli,- the sun god. who was their chief god.

Our Lady's feet rest on a crescent moon which is supported by a winged angel. This convinced the Aztecs of Mary's dominance over darkness and her power over the Aztec moon goddess, Coyolxauhqui.

Mary's star-studded cloak was seen as a sign that she had come down to earth from Heaven. Its design reveals a picture of the night sky as it was on December 12, 1531. The view is not looking up from earth, but looking down from space.

Some symbols show Mary's identification with the native people, such as the predominantly olive color of her skin, her free-flowing hair (the sign of an Aztec woman's virginity), and the black ribbon around her waist (the sign of pregnancy).

Although the image contains many other symbols, Mary's downcast eyes and hands folded in prayer represent her humility, and of special significance is the medallion she is wearing around her neck. It is engraved with a cross, proclaiming her consecration to Jesus.

In 1979, Dr. Philip Callahan, a biophysicist at the University of Florida, stated that the image of Our Lady of Guadalupe is impossible to reproduce because the composition of its colors is unknown. He also said that the fabric on which the image appears should have disintegrated centuries ago because of its being subjected to all kinds of atmospheric conditions.[7]

---

[6] "A great sign appeared in the sky, a woman clothed with the sun, with the moon under her feet, and on her head a crown of twelve stars." (Rev. 12:1).

[7] Sennott, Br. Thomas Mary. "The Tilma of Guadalupe: A Scientific Analysis." <u>The Miracle Hunter</u>: "Marian Apparitions." http://www.miraclehunter.com/marian_apparitions/approved_apparitions/ guadalupe/article_11.html

Since 1979, Dr. José Aste Tonsmann of The Mexican Center of Guadalupean Studies has been examining Mary's eyes. Using digitalized high-resolution imagery to magnify her pupils 2,500 times, he was able to see what Mary saw in the bishop's reception room: a bearded Juan Diego with a full head of hair (outlined in red in the left image below), and the presence of at least 13 other people (in the right image below).[8]

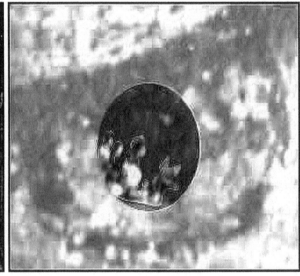

In August 2017, NASA scientists examined the image. They found that characteristic of all humans, the pupils in Mary's eyes became smaller at the approach of light and larger when light receded.

The team also discovered two additional inexplicable facts. The first is that regardless of seasonal temperature change, the image remained at 98.6 degrees Fahrenheit, the norm for a human being. Their second finding was that a stethoscope placed in the area of Mary's womb detected a pulse rate of 115 beats per minute, the typical heartbeat of an unborn child.[9]

---

[8.]"What's to be seen by looking into Our Lady of Guadalupe's eyes?" https://aleteia.org/2016/11/07/whats-to-be-seen-by-looking-into-our-lady-of-guadalupes-eyes/.

[9.] "NASA has called the image of the Virgin of Guadalupe living." August 2017. https://www.matrixdrops.com/en/news/nasa-has-called-the-image-of-the-virgin-of-guadalupe-living/

In its nearly 500-year exposure to the elements, the colors of the image have not faded, the tilma has not disintegrated, and Our Lady's skin has not aged. The image is not a painting for there are no brushstrokes, nor is it a camera shot since photography had not yet been invented. This is the only picture we have of the Blessed Mother. It is truly beyond scientific explanation.

For a visual presentation of the image, see the 22-minute Vaticancatholic.com video, **The Amazing and Miraculous Story of Our Lady of Guadalupe** at www.YouTube.com

# c. <u>Of Added Interest</u>
## <u>The Image of Our Lady of Guadalupe in History</u>

1. Personally aware of the many miracles attributed to the intercession of Our Lady of Guadalupe, Bishop Zumárraga (the first bishop of Mexico and the prelate before whom Juan Diego appeared) had a copy of Our Lady's image made. It was then touched to the original and sent to King Philip II of Spain.

2. When Spain's famous Imperial Admiral, Andrea Doria, retired at the age of 89, he gave his title to his grandnephew, Giovanni Andrea Doria (who was then called .by his granduncle's name, Andrea Doria). The new admiral's inheritance included command of all of Spain's unparalleled naval forces. Because of the threat of an imminent all-out attack by Moslem invaders, Pope St. Pius V formed "The Holy League" for Catholics who would fight to defend Christendom. The participating members supplied a fleet of ships under the command of King Philip's illegitimate half-brother, Don John of Austria. Before the October 7, 1571, historic Battle of Lepanto, Philip asked Andrea Doria to place the image of Our Lady of Guadalupe aboard his flagship. The image, together with a blessed Rosary which each man carried, and the Pope's request that all Catholics pray the Rosary for the Blessed Mother's intercession, resulted in a stunning Catholic victory,[10] which put an end to Moslem attempts to invade Europe by sea.

---

[10.]To commemorate the occasion, Pope St. Pius V declared a feast day called "Feast of Our Lady of Victory." In 1573, Pope Gregory XIII changed the name to Feast of the Holy Rosary." Pope Leo XIII then changed the title in 1895 to "Queen of the Most Holy Rosary." In 1913, Pope Pius X changed the feast day from the first Sunday in October to October 7, the date of the decisive Battle of Lepanto. In 1960, Pope John XXIII gave us the title we use today: "Feast of Our Lady of the Rosary.

3. Our Lady of Guadalupe was canonically crowned by Pope Leo XIII in 1895.

4. In the 20th century, two attempts were made to destroy Juan Diego's tilma, which was and still is on public display in the Basilica of Our Lady of Guadalupe in Mexico City.

    a. The first attempt took place in 1929 with the explosion of 29 sticks of dynamite which had been placed in a vase of roses in front of the tilma. Although there was a lot of damage to the surrounding area, including the twisted. metal of a bronze altar crucifix, the tilma was unharmed.

    b. In 1951, a second attempt was also unsuccessful because the. bomb, which had been planted near the tilma, failed to explode.

5. In 1946, Pope Pius XII (1939-1958) declared **Our Lady of Guadalupe "Patroness of the Americas."**

6. The feast day of **Our Lady of Guadalupe** is December 12.

# 3. <u>OUR LADY OF LOURDES</u>

# The Story

In 1858, in Lourdes, France, the Blessed Mother appeared 18 times to a 14-year-old peasant girl named Bernadette Soubirous.

Our Lady encouraged Bernadette to come to the Grotto of Massabieille each day with a blessed candle and recite the Rosary[1] for the conversion of sinners. The "beautiful lady" led the girl to a miraculous spring that suddenly came out of the ground and told her to drink and bathe in its water. She also instructed Bernadette to tell the bishop that she wanted him to build a chapel where she had appeared and to conduct processions in honor of the Blessed Mother. Although Bernadette kept asking the "beautiful lady" who she was, it wasn't until her 16th appearance that Mary identified herself: "I am the Immaculate Conception."[2]

Lourdes is one of the most popular places of pilgrimage for people who suffer from all kinds of infirmities. They come to bathe in the water and participate in the nightly processions in honor of Our Lady. Although untold thousands have sought healing, fewer than 75 physical cures have officially been declared miraculous.

---

[1.] The Rosary consists of a litany of prayers which recall memorable events in the lives of Jesus and the Blessed Mother. It is the most popular devotion in the Roman Catholic Church.

[2.] "I am the Immaculate Conception" means that Mary was born without original sin so that Jesus could enter her womb and come into the world in human form.

Four years earlier, in 1854, Pope Pius IX (1846-1878) had proclaimed "*ex cathedra*" ("from the chair of St. Peter," the first pope) the doctrine of Mary's Immaculate Conception as being divinely true.

In 1950, Pope Pius XII (1939-1958) declared a second doctrine about Mary. It is called the Assumption and it states that when the Blessed Mother left this world, she went straight to Heaven - body and soul.

These two doctrines about Mary are among the **infallible** teachings of the Roman Catholic Church.

# 4. <u>OUR LADY OF FATIMA</u>

## a. <u>The Story</u>

Among the most recognized visitations of the Blessed Mother are her six appearances to three shepherd children - Lucia dos Santos and her two cousins, Francisco and Jacinta Marto - in Fatima, Portugal, from the 13th of May, 1917 through the 13th of October, 1917. These apparitions occurred during the time of WWI.

At her July 13 appearance, Mary shared three apocalyptic visions and prophecies with the children. They have since been referred to as "The Three Secrets of Fatima." The first was a call to do penance. Our Blessed Mother asked us to make sacrifices to Jesus for the repentance and conversion of sinners and for the reparation of offenses against her Immaculate Heart. She showed the children a terrifying glimpse of Hell where human souls were writhing in agonizing pain as they were being tortured by demons in a setting of smoke and flames.

Mary also taught the children a prayer which she wished to be said after each decade of the Rosary: "O my Jesus, forgive us our sins; save us from the fires of Hell, and lead all souls to Heaven - especially those in most need of Thy mercy."

Mary's second message was a call to pray the Rosary every day for an end to WWI and for an era of peace in the world. She warned that although WWI would end soon,[1] if people did not stop offending God, a more terrible war would break out during the pontificate of Pius XII (1939-1958). This, of course, was WWII.

Mary, the Queen of Heaven, asked that we perform acts of penance for our own sins and for the sins of others. She also requested devotion to her Immaculate Heart to obtain many graces.

In order to stop the spread of the evils of communism, Mary asked that the Pope consecrate Russia to her Immaculate Heart.  Although Russia is not mentioned specifically by name, in 2002, Pope St. John Paul II (1978-2005) consecrated the world to Mary's Immaculate Heart.

Eight years later, Pope Francis (2013 -) consecrated both the world and his pontificate to Mary's Immaculate Heart under the title "Our Lady of Fatima."

---

[1]November 11, 1918

The third secret of Fatima, which was supposed to be made public on Lucia's death or in 1960 (whichever came first), was not revealed until 2000. Its contents are still open to interpretation. Under the vow of obedience, in 1944, Lucia wrote down what the children saw. The vision begins with an angel shouting "Penance, Penance, Penance" and a bishop dressed in white (the Pope?) passing through the section of a large devastated city, which is strewn with corpses. The bishop arrives at a mountain which has a huge wooden cross on its summit. Accompanied by a procession of followers from various walks of life, he begins his ascent. When he gets to the top, soldiers kill him with bullets and arrows. They also kill all the people who are with him. Two angels collect blood from the dead bodies and go down the mountain to anoint the many who are waiting to begin the climb.

Mary told the three shepherd children that on her final visit, October 13, she would reveal who she was and what she wanted. She also said that she would perform a great miracle. This would be **The Miracle of the Sun,**" witnessed by an estimated 70,000 people.

On February 21, 2017, the Fortiternontrepide division of YouTube issued a 27:58 video to commemorate the 100th anniversary of Our Lady's appearances at Fatima. It is called **The Entire Story of Our Lady of Fatima and the Angel**.

---

[1.]**The Entire Story of Our Lady of Fatima and the Angel**. **100**th **year anniversary!!**
  htpps://www.youtube.com/watch?v=RxZBxEJz1v8

### b. *"The Miracle of the Sun"*

This scene, which was photographed and printed in newspapers all over the world, shows people looking directly at a dancing sun without fear of damaging their eyes, Then, without warning, the sun became a wildly spinning disc headed to crash into the earth. Expressions of terror appeared on people's faces; some men and women began screaming; others started praying. Then suddenly, the sun stopped gyrating and returned to its normal state.

(While **"The Miracle of the Sun"** was unfolding, Lucia, Francisco, and Jacinta were experiencing an apparition of the Blessed Mother accompanied by St. Joseph and Jesus).

Since the time of these events at Fatima, Our Lady has consistently appeared all over the world with the same message: "Stop offending God and repent before it's too late!"

# C. <u>THE HOLY SPIRIT</u>

## 1. <u>A Brief History</u>

Despite the Fall, Our Creator has never abandoned us. He has, in fact, consistently provided ways to help us re-enter His kingdom. In the Old Testament, for example, He gave us a spiritual instruction manual called "The Ten Commandments." In the New Testament, He sent His Son (Jesus) to sacrifice His life in atonement for our sins, and Jesus promised that He would send us the Holy Spirit with special gifts and blessings.

It was on the actual feast day of Shavuoth/Pentecost,[1] which occurred shortly after Jesus had ascended to Heaven, that the apostles were gathered together

> And suddenly there came from the sky a noise like a strong driving wind, and it filled the entire house in which they were. Then there appeared to them tongues as of fire which parted and came to rest on each one of them.
> And they were all filled with the Holy Spirit and began to speak in different tongues as the Spirit enabled them to proclaim. (Acts 2:2-4)

> And Jesus appeared to the apostles, saying,
> "Peace be with you; 'As the Father sent me, so am I sending you.' Then He breathed on them and said: 'Receive the Holy Spirit. If you forgive anyone's sins, they are forgiven; if you retain anyone's sins, they are retained.'" (John 20:21-23)

These words are mind-boggling! Imagine! The Lord of the Universe is giving certain human beings divine power to forgive or not forgive sins!

---

[1] The feast of Shavuoth (Hebrew: meaning "seven weeks") is known to Christians as Pentecost (Greek: meaning "50 days"). Both names refer to the period of time between the Exodus and God's gift of "The Ten Commandments" to Moses and the Israelites on Mount Sinai. Shavuoth/Pentecost was one of the three major grain festivals, which required Jews to go on pilgrimage to Jerusalem to make an offering at the Temple in thanksgiving for their harvest.

As a result of all the commotion, a large crowd had assembled outside. Peter then stood up and spoke about Jesus. The pilgrims were astonished that they were able to understand his words in their own language.

On that day[1] some 3,000 Jews accepted Jesus as their Messiah. (Acts 2: 5+)

## When God spoke, they listened!

---

[1] Because of the miraculous appearance of the Holy Spirit, Pentecost is considered the birthday of the Church.

## 2. <u>The Charismatic Renewal</u>

In February 1967, a group of college students was praying together on a weekend retreat at Duquesne University in Pittsburgh, Pennsylvania when they suddenly experienced an outpouring of the gifts of the Holy Spirit. Like the apostles, their lives were immediately changed. They were so filled with God's love that they were impelled to tell everyone what God had done for them.

This event was the beginning of the Charismatic[1] Movement. Prayer groups began to spring up all over the country, as well as abroad. Since then, millions of people have been "baptized in the Spirit" and have given witness to the power of God in their lives.

Once again, we are reminded of the words of St. Paul in his letter to the Romans (5:5): "The love of God has been poured into our hearts through the Holy Spirit[2] Who has been given to us."

---

[1] The word "charismatic" comes from the Greek word "charisma," which means "gift." Here it refers to the gifts of the Holy Spirit.

[2] 1 Corinthians 12:7-11.
  7. To each individual the manifestation of the Spirit is given for some benefit.
  8. To one is given through the Spirit the expression of wisdom; to another the expression of knowledge according to the same Spirit;
  9. To another faith by the same Spirit; to another gifts of healing by the one Spirit;
  10. To another mighty deeds; to another prophecy; to another discernment of spirits; to another varieties of tongues; to another interpretation of tongues.
  11. But one and the same Spirit produces all of these, distributing them individually to each person as He wishes.

# D. THE STIGMATA

## 1. A Brief Description

Another inexplicable way God reveals Himself is through the stigmata, the five agonizing wounds[1] which Jesus endured during His crucifixion. These signs of Christ's ordeal also manifest themselves in "victim souls," individuals who are so inflamed with the love of God that they have been specially chosen to unite their suffering with Jesus' suffering for the reparation of sins and the conversion of sinners. One or more of the stigmatic's visible or invisible wounds can cause excruciating pain. When the visible ones bleed, it is said that they exude a perfumed sweetness.

The first recorded stigmatic was St. Francis of Assisi (1181-1226).

---

[1]·Two in His hands, two in His feet, and one in His side.

# 2. St. Padre Pio

In the 20th century, the most famous stigmatic was, undoubtedly, St. Padre Pio (1887-1968). Known as the "Miracle Worker" and canonized in 2002, St. Pio, who had "the odor of sanctity," was the first known priest to receive the stigmata. He wore gloves when he said Mass because his hands would bleed at the consecration.

Among his many extraordinary gifts, St. Pio was known for his ability to "read souls," levitate, bilocate, and understand languages he didn't know.

On May 5, 1956, he said the opening Mass at La Casa Sollievo della Sofferenza (The Home for the Relief of Suffering), the hospital he founded in San Giovanni Rotondo, Italy.

St. Padre Pio

[1]Brockhaus, Hannah. "The Hospital on a Hill: Padre Pio's Earthly Work." 7/20/2018. https://www.catholicnewsagency.com/news/38906/the-hospital-on-a-hill-padre-pios-earthly-work

# 3. **Blessed Anne Catherine Emmerich**

Another famous stigmatic is Blessed Anne Catherine Emmerich (1774-1824), an Augustinian nun, visionary,[1] and author of a number of spiritual books about Jesus, Mary, and the Rosary.[2] In addition to the stigmata, Blessed Anne also suffered the pain of Christ's crown of thorns.[3]

Blessed Anne's devotion to the Eucharist was so great that for more than ten years, the Eucharist was her only food and water was her only drink.

Blessed Anne Catherine Emmerich

---

[1] It was in a vision that Blessed Anne discovered the house in which the Blessed Mother and St. John the Evangelist lived in Ephesus (once a major Greek city, which is now in present day Turkey).
The house was found in the 19th century by following her directions.

[2] Clemens Brentano, the German poet and novelist, visited Anne on a more or less regular basis.

[3] In her book *The Dolorous Passion of Our Lord Jesus Christ,* Blessed Anne details her vision of being present in Jerusalem when Jesus was arrested on Holy Thursday and made to suffer the tortuous cruelty which followed.
Mel Gibson used scenes from this book in his movie *The Passion of the Christ.* (2004).

# PART V

## DEVELOPING A PERSONAL RELATIONSHIP WITH GOD

**LESSON:** Saying "Yes" to God Calls for **SPIRITUAL GROWTH through**

**A. WORSHIP** - The Mass is the most important worship service in the Roman Catholic Church for it is within its structure that consecrated bread and wine are transformed into the body and blood of Our Lord Jesus Christ.

**B. PRAYER** - a lifting of the mind, heart, and spirit to the Divine

Basically, there are four types of prayer:

### 1. Types of Prayer

    a. Adoration - praising God and all heavenly creatures

    b. Petition - asking for something

    c. Thanksgiving - expressing gratitude

    d. Contrition - saying you're sorry

### 2. Some Special Prayers

    **a. "Our Father"**

Our Father, Who art in Heaven,

Hallowed be Thy name.

Thy kingdom come,

Thy will be done on earth

As it is in Heaven.

Give us this day our daily bread

And forgive us our trespasses

As we forgive those

Who trespass against us.

And lead us not into temptation,

But deliver us from evil,

For Thine is the kingdom,

And the power, and the glory

Forever. Amen.

56

### b. "*Hail Mary*"

Hail Mary, full of grace;

The Lord is with thee.

Blessed art thou among women, and

Blessed is the fruit of thy womb, Jesus!

Holy Mary, Mother of God,

Pray for us sinners

Now and at the hour of our death.

Amen.

### c. "*Glory Be*"

Glory be to the Father, the Son,

And the Holy Spirit,

As it was in the beginning,

Is now,

And ever shall be -

World without end.

Amen.

### d. "*The Divine Praises*"

Blessed be God.

Blessed be His Holy Name.

Blessed be Jesus Christ, true God and true man.

Blessed be the Name of Jesus.

Blessed be His Most Sacred Heart.

Blessed be His Most Precious Blood.

Blessed be Jesus in the Most Holy Sacrament of the Altar.

Blessed be the Holy Spirit, the Paraclete.

Blessed be the great Mother of God, Mary most Holy.

Blessed be her holy and Immaculate Conception.

Blessed be her glorious Assumption.

Blessed be the name of Mary, Virgin and Mother.

Blessed be St. Joseph, her most chaste spouse.

Blessed be God in His Angels and in His Saints.

May the heart of Jesus, in the Most Blessed Sacrament, be praised, adored, and loved with grateful affection, at every moment, in all the tabernacles of the world, even to the end of time. Amen.

# C. DEVOTIONS

## 1. The Rosary

The Rosary is the foremost devotion in honor of the Blessed Mother. It chronicles major events in the lives of Jesus and Mary.

## a. A Brief History

It is believed that the origin of the Rosary goes back to the recitation and chanting of the 150 Biblical psalms by 9th century Irish monks.[1]

St. Dominic (1170-1221) is the person who is most associated with the Rosary. It is said that after receiving an apparition of the Blessed Mother, he dedicated his life to spreading this devotion.

In thanksgiving for the defeat of the Moslems in the October 7, 1571 Battle of Lepanto, Pope St. Pius V declared October 7 a feast day in honor of Our Lady of Victory, and the month of October, the month of the Rosary. In 1573, Pope Gregory XIII changed the name of this feast day to Our Lady of the Rosary.

In 2002. Pope St. John Paul II added the Luminous Mysteries to the centuries old Joyful, Sorrowful, and Glorious Mysteries. He felt that there should be a transition from the last joyful mystery, which focuses on the boy Jesus teaching in the temple, to the first sorrowful mystery, showing the man Jesus in the Garden of Gethsemane, contemplating His forthcoming agony and death.

The Blessed Mother also requested Communions of reparation in atonement for the sins of the world and the offering of the following special prayer for sinners, to be said after each decade of the Rosary:

"O my Jesus, forgive us our sins, save us from the fires of Hell,
Lead all souls to Heaven, especially those in most need of Thy mercy."

In a 1930 visitation to Sister Lucia (one of the Fatima visionaries), Jesus said, "Here then, My Daughter, is the reason why the Immaculate Heart of Mary (My Mother) causes Me to ask for this little act of reparation and by means of it, moves My mercy to forgive those souls who had the misfortune of offending her."

## b. <u>The Joyful Mysteries</u>

(Said on Mondays and Saturdays)

### 1. <u>The Annunciation</u>

The angel Gabriel tells Mary that she will conceive a son by the Holy Spirit.

### 2. <u>The Visitation</u>

Mary goes to stay with her six-months pregnant cousin Elizabeth until the birth of Elizabeth's son, John the Baptist.

### 3. <u>The Birth of Our Lord</u>

Mary gives birth to Jesus in a stable in the town of Bethlehem.

### 4. <u>The Presentation of Baby Jesus in the Temple</u>

In accordance with the covenant God made with Moses, Jesus is named and circumcised.

### 5. <u>The Finding of the Boy Jesus in the Temple</u>

Missing for three days, Jesus is found in the Temple teaching the Elders the meaning of various Biblical passages.

## c. <u>The Luminous Mysteries</u>

(Said on Thursdays)

### 1. <u>The Baptism of Jesus</u>

Jesus was an adult when He was baptized in the Jordan River by His cousin John the Baptist.

### 2. Jesus Performs His First Public Miracle at Cana

Jesus' first public miracle was to change water into wine at a wedding feast.

### 3. The Proclamation of the Kingdom

Jesus' public ministry included performing cures, preaching repentance and conversion, and forgiving sins.

### 4. The Transfiguration

Jesus took Peter and the brothers James and John to the top of a mountain. When Moses and Elijah appeared, He began conversing with them and became as radiant as the sun.

### 5. The Institution of the Eucharist

On Holy Thursday at the "Last Supper," Jesus transformed bread and wine into His body and blood.

## d. The Sorrowful Mysteries

(Said on Tuesdays and Fridays)

### 1. The Agony in the Garden

Jesus struggles with accepting the will of God the Father.

### 2. The Scourging at the Pillar

Jesus suffers physical abuse at the hands of the Roman guards.

### 3. The Crowning with Thorns

Jesus suffers pain and humiliation from the Roman guards.

### 4. The Carrying of the Cross

Jesus is mocked and jeered at by the people who came to watch Him suffer and die.

### 5. The Crucifixion

Jesus dies after three hours of unbelievable agony.

## e. The Glorious Mysteries

(Said on Wednesdays and Sundays)

### 1. The Resurrection

Jesus overcomes death and appears to a number of His followers.

### 2. The Ascension

In the presence of witnesses, 40 days after His resurrection, Jesus leaves the earth by physically rising to Heaven.

### 3. The Descent of the Holy Spirit

50 days after Jesus' Resurrection, the Holy Spirit appears in Jerusalem on the Feast of Weeks (Pentecost) and showers the Apostles with spiritual gifts. (Acts 2:1)

### 4. The Assumption

Mary, Mother of Jesus, is taken up to Heaven, body and soul.

### 5. The Coronation of Mary, Virgin and Mother

Mary is crowned Queen of Heaven.

## 2. The Divine Mercy Chaplet

(Prayer for the forgiveness of sins committed by the person who is praying the chaplet as well as for the forgiveness of sins committed by everyone in the world.

### a. A Brief History

In the 1930s, Our Lord appeared a number of times to Sr. Faustina, an uneducated nun in a convent in Poland, with a message of forgiveness. It is that God loves each one of us and His mercy is greater than our sins.

## b. Presentation

The Chaplet is prayed on a five-decade Rosary. It begins with the Sign of the Cross: "In the name of the Father, and of the Son, and of the Holy Spirit. Amen." and is followed by the "Our Father," the "Hail Mary," and

## "The Apostle's Creed"

"I believe in God, the Father Almighty, Creator of Heaven and earth, and in Jesus Christ, His only Son, our Lord, Who was conceived by the Holy Spirit, born of the Virgin Mary, suffered under Pontius Pilate, was crucified, died, and was buried. He descended into Hell and on the third day He rose again from the dead; He ascended into Heaven and is seated at the right hand of God the Father Almighty; from there He will come to judge the living and the dead.

I believe in the Holy Spirit, the Holy Catholic Church, the communion of saints, the forgiveness of sins, the resurrection of the body, and life everlasting. Amen."

The "Eternal Father" prayer is then recited on the large bead of the first decade:

> "Eternal Father, I (we) offer you the Body and Blood,
> Soul and Divinity of Your Dearly Beloved Son, Our Lord
> Jesus Christ, in atonement for my (our} sins and those of
> the whole world."

The "Eternal Father" prayer is followed by:

> "For the sake of His sorrowful passion, have mercy on me (us)
> and on the whole world.".

This pattern is repeated for the remaining four decades. The Divine Mercy Chaplet ends with three recitations of the "Holy God" prayer:

> "Holy God, Holy Mighty One, Holy Immortal One, have mercy on me (us)
> and on the whole world."

### 3. <u>Novenas</u>

Nine[1] consecutive days of offering prayers, Masses, and/or sacrifices for a special intention.

### 4. <u>First Fridays</u>[2]

Nine consecutive months of attending Mass and receiving Communion to honor the Sacred Heart of Jesus.

### 5. <u>First Saturdays</u>[3]

Five consecutive months of attending Mass and receiving Communion in reparation for offenses committed against the Immaculate Heart of Mary.[4]

---

[1] Why nine? One theory is that nine represents the number of months Jesus spent in Mary's womb.

[2] **First Fridays**: Jesus appeared to St. Margaret Mary Alacoque (1643-1690) with 12 promises of heavenly rewards to the faithful who participate in this devotion.

[3] **First Saturdays**: In her July 13, 1917 appearance at Fatima, the Blessed Mother said:

> "I promise to assist at the hour of death with the graces necessary for salvation all those who, in order to make reparation to me, on the First Saturday of five successive months, go to confession, receive Holy Communion, say five decades of the Rosary, and keep me company for a quarter of an hour, meditating on the fifteen (twenty since 2002) mysteries of the Rosary."

[4] Guido Del Rose analyzes **The Five Sins Against Our Lady of Fatima**. Mar 13, 2006.
http://www.catholictradition.org/Mary/fatima2a.htm

## D. ATTENDING RELIGIOUS EVENTS

1. Days of Recollection
2. Retreats
3. Talks
4. Conferences
5. Courses

## E. READING SPIRITUAL BOOKS, INCLUDING

## *THE BIBLE*

## F. JOINING A PARISH ORGANIZATION

## G. HAVING RELIGIOUS FRIENDS

# PART VI
## AFTERTHOUGHTS

Initially, you and I did not choose to love God: God chose to love us. He called each one of us by name and said, "I want you to live your life in My love so that I can give you eternal happiness."

When the angel Gabriel appeared to Mary, saying, "The Holy Spirit will come upon you, and the power of the Most High will overshadow you," (Luke 1:36) she replied, "Behold, I am the handmaid of the Lord. May it be done to me according to your word." (Luke 1:38)

When Jesus called the apostles, they immediately stopped what they were doing and followed Him.

God continues to communicate with His people in different ways. Right now, the fact that you are reading these words suggests that God may be speaking to **you** –

## AND

## *WHEN GOD SPEAKS, YOU BETTER LISTEN!*

# PART VII
# REFERENCES

Acutis, Carlo. **Eucharistic Miracles of the World**.
  **http://www.miracolieucaristici.org/**

Brockhaus, Hannah. "The Hospital on a Hill: Padre Pio's Earthly Work."
  **https://www.catholicnewsagency.com/news/38906/the-hospital-on-a-hill-padre-pios-earthly-work/** July 20, 2018.

"In Memoriam: Frederick T. Zugibe" (Sept. 6, 2013). Haverstraw, NY:
  The Journal News.

Kioska, Robert. "Why Did Nine Million People Suddenly Turn Catholic?"
  Thoughts from the Side of the House. January 23, 2017.
  **https://www.sideofthehouse.blog/2017/01/**

**Miracle of Lanciano Medical Report by Dr. Linoli. [VIDEO] 9/4/2020.**
  **https://www.youtube.com/watch?v=OaoaHNhX1pk**

"NASA has called the image of the Virgin of Guadalupe living." August 2017.
  **http://www.matrixdrops.com/en/news/nasa-has-called-the-image-of-the-virgin-of-guadalupe-living/**

Pope Francis, **Eucharistic Miracle in Buenos Aires, Argentina (1996)**.
  **https://www.absoluteprimacyofchrist.org/pope-francis-eucharistic-miracle-in-buenos-aires-argentina/**   Posted March 28, 2013.

Rudden, Dan. "A Brief History of the Rosary." The Rosary Foundation.
  **http://www.erosary.com/rosary/about/history**

Sennott, Br. Thomas Mary. "The Tilma of Guadalupe: A Scientific Analysis."
The Miracle Hunter: "Marian Apparitions."
http://www.miraclehunter.com/marian_apparitions/approved_apparitions/
guadalupe/article_11.html

**The Amazing and Miraculous Image of Our Lady of Guadalupe.** [Video].
https://www.youtube.com/watch?v=xe4Ozm0oENk

**The Entire Story of Our Lady of Fatima and the Angel. 100th year anniversary!!**
https://www.youtube.com/watch?v=RxZBxEJz1v8

**"The Five Sins Against Our Lady."** Guido Del Rose. Mar 13, 2006.
https://www.traditioninaction.org/religious/a019rpFiveSins_GuidoDelRose.htm
**(An edited version of Guido Del Rose's Article: "Fatima: The Five Sins.")**

The Miracle of Lanciano. [VIDEO] 4/17/2011.
https://www.youtube.com/watch?v=whbzLYi7cyc

*The New American Bible, Revised Edition (NABRE).*
Washington, DC: Confraternity of Christian Doctrine, Inc., 2010.

"What's to be seen by looking into Our Lady of Guadalupe's eyes?"
https://aleteia.org/2016/11/07/whats-to-be-seen-by-looking-into-our-lady-
of-Guadalupes-eyes/

# About the Author

With her all-encompassing background as a teacher, composer, author, editor, and speaker, Nan Clark's books are as diversified as her talents.

## Published Works

***When God Speaks, You Better Listen!*** focuses on human encounters with the Divine.

***The Promise*** tells the story of Beatrice Castiglia-Catullo, the recently deceased 101½-year-old founder of **R.A.I.N.**, one of New York City's largest non-profit service organizations for senior citizens.

***MAGNIFICAT PUNS*** challenges the reader to use visual and text clues to come up with 50 descriptive titles containing the word "Cat" or a word related to "Cat."

***The World's Greatest Star Trek Quiz*** commemorates the 30th anniversary of the original TV series.

***Play Time*** presents 10 piano solos for Late-Elementary to Early-Intermediate students.